THE JAMESTOWN COLONY DISASTER

BY MARCIA AMIDON LUSTED

A CAUSE-AND-EFFECT
INVESTIGATION

CAUSE + EFFECT
DISASTERS

LERNER PUBLICATIONS ◆ MINNEAPOLIS

Lerner Publications Company
A division of Lerner Publishing Group, Inc.
241 First Avenue North
Minneapolis, MN 55401 USA

For reading levels and more information, look up this title at www.lernerbooks.com.

Content Consultant: Mark Summers, Manager, Public and Educational Programs, Jamestown Rediscovery

Library of Congress Cataloging-in-Publication Data

Names: Lusted, Marcia Amidon.
Title: The Jamestown Colony disaster : a cause and effect investigation / by Marcia Amidon Lusted.
Description: Minneapolis : Lerner Publications, 2017. | Series: Cause-and-effect disasters | Audience: Grades 4 to 6. | Includes bibliographical references and index.
Identifiers: LCCN 2016008870 (print) | LCCN 2016016565 (ebook) | ISBN 9781512411164 (library bound : alkaline paper) | ISBN 9781512411270 (eb pdf)
Subjects: LCSH: Jamestown (Va.)—History—17th century—Juvenile literature. | Jamestown (Va.)—Ethnic relations—History—17th century—Juvenile literature. | Disasters—Virginia—Jamestown—History—17th century—Juvenile literature. | Causation—Juvenile literature. | Virginia—History—Colonial period, ca. 1600–1775—Juvenile literature.
Classification: LCC F234.J3 L84 2017 (print) | LCC F234.J3 (ebook) | DDC 975.5/4251—dc23

LC record available at https://lccn.loc.gov/2016008870

Manufactured in the United States of America
1 - VP - 7/15/16

TABLE OF CONTENTS

A NEW START

On December 20, 1606, three ships
sailed from England. Aboard them were
a total of 105 men. The men were traveling
to Virginia in the New World. Once they arrived,
they would establish a settlement there. These explorers were
funded by investors of London's Virginia Company. They hoped to
find precious gold, silver, and other raw materials to send back to
England.

The group arrived in Virginia in April 1607. One man had died
on the journey. The first task for the remaining 104 men was to
choose a site for their new home. By May 1607 they had found a

Men from England
arrived in Virginia
in April 1607.

location. It was 60 miles (97 kilometers) from the mouth of the Chesapeake Bay. The land was surrounded by water on three sides. The water was deep enough to moor their ships. The Spanish had already set up settlements in the New World. This location would be easy to defend against Spanish invasions. It also did not have any existing American Indian settlements. The explorers named the new settlement Jamestown, after their king, James I. It would become the first permanent English settlement in North America.

The site of Jamestown, and the entire region of

Virginia, was not just an empty land. American Indians, including the Powhatan, lived in the area. The Powhatan Confederacy was a group of six tribes. This strong alliance also had influence over about twenty-four other tribes in the region. The area was also home to the Monacan. They were enemies of the Powhatan.

The Powhatan called the land *Tsenacomoco*. This translates as "densely inhabited land," and it was. By the time the English settlers arrived, one supreme chief, also called Powhatan, ruled the area. Through alliances he had increased the size of Tsenacomoco. It was about 8,000 square miles (20,700 square kilometers). Fourteen thousand people lived there. Most of the Powhatan lived in small villages of several hundred people.

The settlers wanted to avoid upsetting Powhatan and his people. So they picked a site for Jamestown away from the other villages. But the Powhatan had a good reason not to use this

Members of the Powhatan tribes may have watched the settlers as they built the Jamestown fort.

land for a village. The site was marshy. There was no fresh water. Mosquitoes infested the area. It was, however, the Powhatan's traditional hunting land.

The American Indians first viewed the English settlers with suspicion. Earlier Spanish explorers had been hostile. The Powhatan attacked the first landing party of Jamestown settlers. But later they offered the English cornbread and other gifts. Chief Powhatan wanted the settlers to join the other communities. Some of the settlers saw the Powhatan as potential trading partners. They hoped to trade for food. Others wanted to use American Indians as slaves and workers.

After choosing the site, the settlers got to work building their settlement. They unloaded tools and supplies. They began clearing trees. They also opened a secret list of orders from the Virginia Company's Royal Council. It gave the names of the men chosen for the settlement's new ruling council. Christopher Newport had been chosen as the admiral of the expedition. The other leaders included Edward Wingfield, Bartholomew Gosnold, and John Smith.

The fence surrounding the Jamestown fort has been recreated for visitors.

JAMESTOWN FORT IN 1607

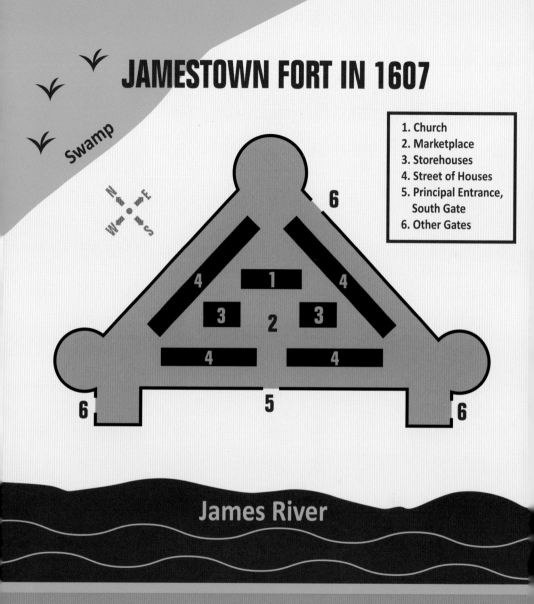

Swamp

1. Church
2. Marketplace
3. Storehouses
4. Street of Houses
5. Principal Entrance, South Gate
6. Other Gates

James River

The settlement was finished by June 15, 1607. It was triangular in shape. Its log fence surrounded a storehouse, church, and houses. At the corners were raised platforms for cannons. They would be used to defend against attacks.

It seemed that the settlers were off to a good start. In a report sent back to London, the council wrote, "Within less than seven weeks, we are fortified well against the Indians; we have sown [a] good store of wheat . . . we have built some houses; we have spared some hands [for exploration]."

But things had already started to go badly. The settlers' relationship with the Powhatan was strained. The English settlers often stole what they wanted instead of trading. The Powhatan fought back with attacks on people and crops. The settlers would soon discover that being poor neighbors led to trouble.

POOR NEIGHBORS

The Jamestown settlers were a mixed group. Of the original party, forty men were soldiers. Thirty-five were considered gentlemen. These were rich men who did not have to work. Most of them were trained as soldiers. In English culture, gentlemen were not expected to work as laborers. The rest of the men were craftsmen, such as blacksmiths, carpenters, and bricklayers, or laborers. Laborers did jobs needing few special skills. They grew crops and helped build houses.

The original goal of the settlement was to find gold and silver. It was not planned as a permanent settlement with families. So there were no women among the settlers. The company's organizers in London had told the settlers that they would send more supplies only if the settlers sent back wealth. The organizers knew that Spanish explorers had found gold in the New World. They expected the same from the Jamestown settlers. As a result, many of the Jamestown men spent their time searching for gold.

Only certain men in the Jamestown group would do manual labor.

The gentlemen in the group did not want to work like laborers. They felt this work was below them. The first supply ship from England wasn't due to arrive until January 1608. Still, the men spent little time planting crops or storing food. They had already received food from the American Indians as a welcome. They thought they could continue to trade for food throughout the winter.

At first, the Powhatan traded food in exchange for metal and English manufactured goods. This partnership helped the Jamestown settlers survive their first winter. Still, many of the settlers were ill from diseases such as typhoid and dysentery. These diseases probably came from drinking dirty river water or water from wells. This water contained *E. coli* bacteria from human or animal waste. The water supply was also partly salt water, which

The settlers were searching for gold in the New World.

Disease-spreading mosquitoes were common in the swampy area of Jamestown.

only makes the drinker thirstier. The location of the settlement was unhealthful, too. Mosquitoes in the swampy area carried the disease malaria.

Powhatan and his people had helped the settlers. But in the fall and winter of 1608 the Powhatan became reluctant to trade food. There had been a drought in the area. This limited the corn supply. They needed to feed themselves.

Captain John Smith tried to negotiate with Chief Powhatan. Smith had come to Jamestown with the other settlers. On the way there, he was accused of mutiny and imprisoned. But when the settlers arrived in Jamestown, they discovered that Smith had been named as one of the members of the ruling council. Eventually, he became the president of the settlement. His strong leadership helped it survive. But he had worked as a soldier before coming to Jamestown. Some of the gentlemen did not like him.

Still, Smith was good at negotiating for food. Powhatan agreed to trade corn for an English house and other gifts from the settlers. But when Smith provided the gifts, Powhatan was not satisfied. Powhatan felt that the English were roaming beyond their territory. They were demanding that Powhatan's people give them food and work without pay. Powhatan told Smith that he had little corn to trade. He would trade one bushel of corn for every English sword that the settlers gave him.

John Smith traveled through Europe, Russia, and Northern Africa before coming to the New World.

Smith did not agree to these terms. After nearly being killed, first by Powhatan and then by another chief, Smith and his men stole some corn and escaped. They returned to the Jamestown fort. The settlers were now at war.

The Virginia Company had ordered Smith to develop good relationships with the American Indians. Now Smith felt it was impossible. He believed the Powhatan could not be trusted. Also, the English and the American Indians had very different ideas of land ownership and government. Smith decided that the only

One settler described Chief Powhatan as "a goodly old man, not yet shrinking" with age.

way to make sure Jamestown had food was to take it by force. The English raided American Indian villages. Sometimes they burned crops that they could not take. They destroyed villages. They hurt or killed the people living there. Powhatan said that the English had invaded his country. To fight back, his warriors began attacking settlers. They also killed livestock and burned crops in the fields.

Smith made changes to keep the colony alive. He created a new rule: no work, no food. Even the gentlemen of Jamestown

The settlers faced attacks from the Powhatan.

had to work like the regular laborers. This made Smith even more unpopular with these men.

In September 1608 a second supply ship arrived from England. It carried food, but also more people to feed. The settlers made it through a few winter months. But by late winter, much of their supply of corn was rotten or had been eaten by rats. The Jamestown settlers could no longer trade for food. How would they survive?

A SERIES OF DISASTERS

In the summer of 1609, nine ships departed England for Jamestown. They were carrying supplies for the settlers. Also onboard were five hundred immigrants. They would join the settlement. But the boats encountered a hurricane. The lead ship, *Sea Venture*, wrecked off the coast of Bermuda. The other eight ships made it. They brought about 350 starving people, including women and children, to Jamestown.

The *Sea Venture* wrecked off the coast of Bermuda on July 28, 1609, on its way to Jamestown.

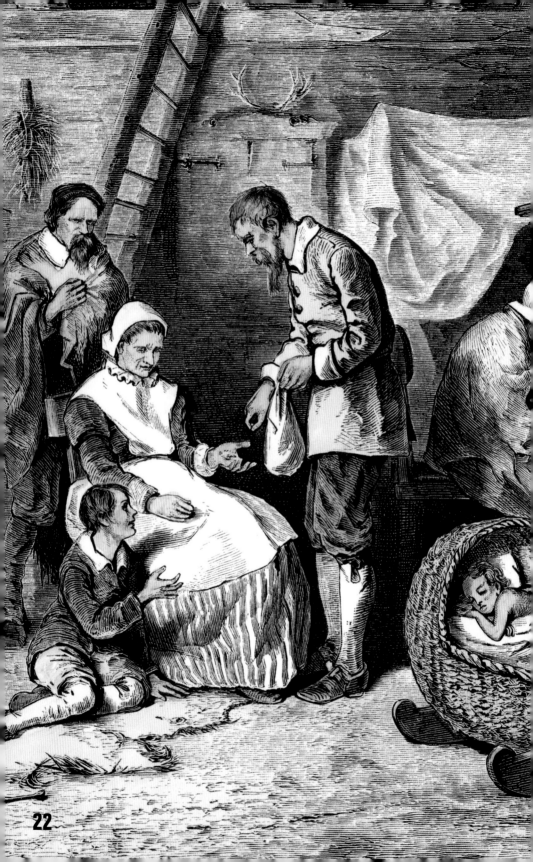

Those in Jamestown thought that all on board the *Sea Venture* had been killed. This included passenger Sir Thomas Gates. Gates had been sent by the Virginia Company to act as governor. He was to replace Smith as the leader of Jamestown. Then, in September, Smith was hurt in a gunpowder explosion, which may or may not have been an accident. He was replaced by George Percy, a gentleman.

By the fall of 1609 the situation was bleak. The food that had been stored for the winter had already been eaten. It was only November. The hundreds of Jamestown settlers were hungry. Percy tried to negotiate with Powhatan and his people but failed. The settlers could no longer trade for corn. The settlement had survived lean times and hard winters before. But in the winter of 1609–1610, it faced disaster.

One Jamestown settler, who returned to England, reported that "[the settlers] fell into extreame want, not having anything left to sustain them save a little ill conditioned Barley, which ground to meal & pottage made thereof, one smale

Unable to trade with the Powhatan, settlers divided out small amounts of food.

23

ladle full was allowed each person for a meale." This terrible winter became known as the Starving Time.

Faced with starvation, some of the people in Jamestown began to eat whatever they could to stay alive. They started with the horses. Then they ate the pigs, chickens, dogs, and cats of the settlement. They grew even more desperate as the days passed. The settlers began eating rats, mice, and snakes. Then they ate any toadstools and mushrooms they could find. Percy wrote, "To satisfy cruel hunger [the settlers were forced] to eat boots, shoes, or any other leather some could come by." But things got even worse. Some settlers began eating human waste. Some even ate the corpses of those who had died and been buried.

The Jamestown settlers were too weak to help themselves. But in May 1610, the crew and passengers from the *Sea Venture*, who everyone had assumed were dead, arrived in Jamestown. They had built two ships from the *Sea Venture*'s wreckage. Among the survivors was Gates. Gates immediately saw the horrible condition of the fort and the settlers. He did not have enough supplies to feed the starving Jamestown settlers. So he decided to take them all back to England. Gates ordered the fort abandoned. He had the settlers bury the fort's cannon and other large weapons. This would keep them from falling into the hands of the American Indians or the Spanish. Gates's group loaded what few things the settlers still had onto ships.

But as their ships began to move down the James River toward the sea, they met a longboat. On board was a messenger from the new colony governor, Lord Delaware. He had just arrived in the nearby Chesapeake Bay with a fleet of ships and supplies. Delaware's messenger ordered the colonists to return to Jamestown. Delaware arrived there the next day.

With the arrival of 150 people from England, as well as food and weapons, things changed for the colonists. They began waging a war against the American Indians who had attacked them. Known as the First Anglo-Powhatan War, it lasted for five years. The English burned towns and villages. They executed women and children as well as warriors.

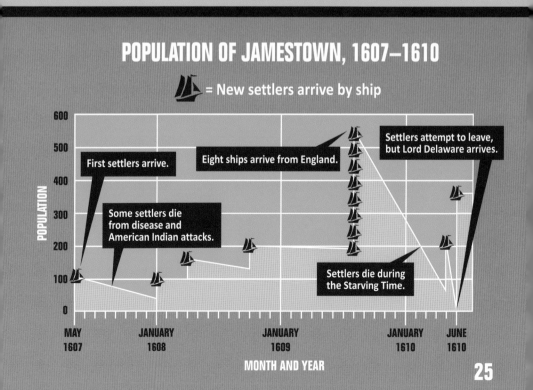

POPULATION OF JAMESTOWN, 1607–1610

= New settlers arrive by ship

POPULATION

600
500
400
300
200
100
0

First settlers arrive.

Some settlers die from disease and American Indian attacks.

Eight ships arrive from England.

Settlers attempt to leave, but Lord Delaware arrives.

Settlers die during the Starving Time.

MAY 1607   JANUARY 1608   JANUARY 1609   JANUARY 1610   JUNE 1610

MONTH AND YEAR

Gradually, Powhatan's forces weakened. English settlers built new settlements along the James River, south of Jamestown. With a better food supply and more settlers to work and defend the colony, they grew stronger. Jamestown settler John Rolfe established a new crop, tobacco. It flourished in the Virginia climate. This could be traded with England for a good price. Rolfe also married Pocahontas. She was the favorite daughter of Chief Powhatan. As an important member of her tribe, she was able to negotiate between the Powhatan and the English settlers.

Things seemed to be finally going well for the English in Virginia. More towns grew up near Jamestown. Africans were brought to Jamestown in 1619. They may have been slaves for the new tobacco plantations. More women arrived from England to be brides for the settlers. Some of the Powhatan came to live in the

After the Starving Time ended, Jamestown began to flourish and expand.

English settlements. But most of the English still treated American Indians as inferior.

The American Indians knew that the English would keep expanding in Virginia. This threatened the Powhatan and their way of life. Some settlers tried to incorporate the Powhatan into English culture. They offered them an English education. They even converted some to Christianity. The Powhatan realized that their own culture was endangered. So Opechancanough, the younger brother of Chief Powhatan and a chief himself, planned a huge attack on the Jamestown fort and the nearby settlements. The attack would later be known as the Massacre of 1622.

On March 21, 1622, Opechancanough's men arrived at the settlements. They brought gifts of meat and fruit. They conducted trading activities. But they were lulling the settlers into thinking

John Rolfe married Pocahontas in 1614.

that relations were good. The next day they turned on the settlers and attacked them. They killed families on plantations and workers in the fields. They burned the plantation buildings, crops, and livestock. They used many of the same brutal tactics that the English had used on the Powhatan before. In all, 347 settlers were killed.

Jamestown heard the news of the attacks before the warriors arrived there. Settlers from surrounding areas fled to the Jamestown fort for safety. They stayed there for several months. The settlers lost valuable crops and supplies in the attack. The fort became overcrowded. But the settlers had once again made themselves too dependent on trading for food. Most of their own land was used to grow tobacco. Many people went hungry and died during the winter of 1622–1623.

The Starving Time and the Massacre of 1622 devastated the settlers. But the hardship was far from over. Even more conflict was in store.

The settlers fought back during the Massacre of 1622 but had to retreat to the fort for safety.

JAMESTOWN SURVIVES 4

In the years following the First Anglo-Powhatan War, relationships between the English settlers and the American Indians did not improve. The English had temporarily left settlements far away from the Jamestown fort. But their leaders felt that the 1622 attack had given the settlers the right to retaliate. They felt that they should no longer try to negotiate with the Powhatan at all.

In the fall of 1622, the colonists launched the Second Anglo-Powhatan War. They attacked villages. They burned or stole the corn crops. During what was supposed to be a peace negotiation, the English offered poisoned drinks to a group of Opechancanough's delegates. This was supposedly to toast the treaty. As the delegates became deathly ill from the poison, the settlers shot them. Settlers continued to attack Powhatan villages. They struck during harvest times. That way, they could carry away corn and grain afterward. But they left just enough for the Powhatan to replant for the next year. This maintained a source of food for the settlers. The English kept the war going for another ten years.

The English took more and more land. Farms spread up and down the James River and beyond. Trade in tobacco and slaves boomed. This brought money to the colony. Nearly eight thousand settlers lived in and around Jamestown.

Even after the war, the English took more land. This threatened the uneasy peace with the people of Tsenacomoco, led by Chief

Opechancanough and his tribe continued trying to stop the settlers from stealing their land and food.

Tobacco crops were very successful in Jamestown.

Opechancanough. On April 18, 1644, the Powhatan led one final attack on the settlers in the Third Anglo-Powhatan War. More than four hundred settlers died. But the settlers killed most of the Powhatan. After Opechancanough was captured and killed, the war ended with a peace treaty. His successor, Necotowance, agreed to the terms. The treaty forced the Powhatan to leave certain areas for the English. They could live only on the north side of the York River.

Settlements around Jamestown continued to grow. Middle Plantation was founded in 1633. It became the capital of the Virginia colony in 1699 and was renamed Williamsburg. The English were now firmly established in the New World. The Tsenacomoco was changing. Years of discrimination and other poor treatment made it hard for the American Indians to survive. But many descendants of the Powhatan Confederacy still live in Virginia, including members of the Pamunkey and Mattaponi tribes.

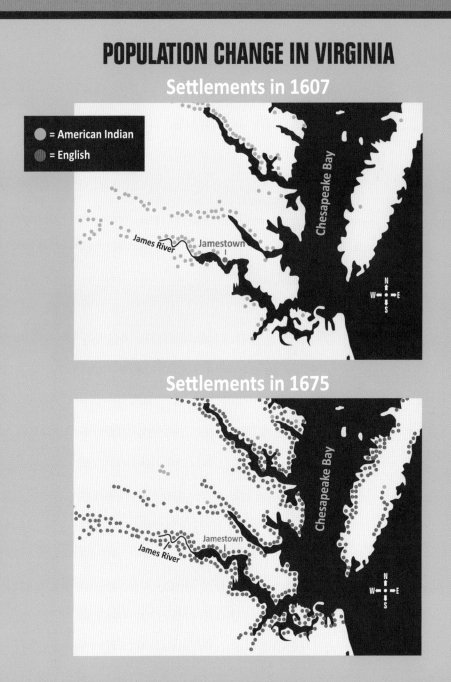

POPULATION CHANGE IN VIRGINIA

Settlements in 1607

= American Indian
= English

James River
Jamestown
Chesapeake Bay

N
W   E
S

Settlements in 1675

Jamestown
James River
Chesapeake Bay

N
W   E
S

Recreations of English and Powhatan homes at Historic Jamestowne show what the colony may have looked like.

The English had made many poor decisions when they started the Jamestown colony. Poor planning, their attitude about the inferiority of American Indians, and their aggressive behavior led to starvation and war. Often, the fate of Jamestown and the Virginia colony hung by a thread. Thousands of people, both English and American Indian, died from starvation and conflict. But despite disasters of their own making, the English established a firm foothold in Jamestown and all of Virginia. They helped make the thirteen colonies that would become the United States of America.

CAUSE

Thirty-five of the original settlers were considered gentlemen.

Trade negotiations between John Smith and Chief Powhatan were unsuccessful. But the settlers were getting desperate for food.

George Percy became the new leader of Jamestown. He was also unable to negotiate with the Powhatan for food.

As the settlers expanded their territory, the Powhatan felt that their way of life was threatened.

The settlers' numbers continued to grow as the tobacco crops and slave trade boomed.

EFFECT

The gentlemen were not used to having to work. They refused to spend time planting crops or storing food.

Smith decided to take food from the Powhatan by force. The Jamestown settlers raided Powhatan villages, killing some of the people.

In the winter of 1609–1610, settlers faced an extreme lack of food. This was called the Starving Time.

The Powhatan launched the Massacre of 1622, killing 347 settlers and destroying crops.

With the increase in numbers, settlers eventually wiped out most of the Powhatan people in wars. A 1644 treaty restricted the Powhatan to areas on the north side of the York River.

Glossary

colony: a place that is under the control of another country, usually far away, and settled by people from that country

confederacy: a group of people or nations joined together for common support

delegate: a person selected to represent a group

drought: a period of time without enough rainfall

hostile: unfriendly or harsh

massacre: a deliberate and violent killing of many people

negotiation: a discussion with the goal of reaching an agreement

plantation: an estate where crops such as tobacco, sugar, and cotton are grown by laborers or slaves who live on that estate

Source Notes

9   Benjamin Woolley, *Savage Kingdom: The True Story of Jamestown, 1607, and the Settlement of America* (New York: HarperCollins Publishers, 2007), 85.

17   "Jamestown," *National Geographic*, May 2007, http://ngm. nationalgeographic.com/2007/05/jamestown/charles-mann-text/2.

23   Ivor Noël Hume, "We Are Starved," *Colonial Williamsburg Journal*, Winter 2007, http://www.history.org/foundation/journal/winter07/starving.cfm.

24   George Percy, "Jamestown: 1609–10: 'Starving Time,'" National Humanities Center, accessed March 4, 2016, http://nationalhumanitiescenter.org/pds/ amerbegin/settlement/text2/JamestownPercyRelation.pdf.

Selected Bibliography

Lepore, Jill. *Encounters in the New World: A History in Documents*. New York: Oxford
    University Press, 2000.

Mann, Charles C. "Colonial Landscapes: America, Lost & Found." *National
    Geographic*. May 2007. http://ngm.nationalgeographic.com/ngm/0705/
    feature1/text2.html

Stebbins, Sarah J. "Pocahontas: Her Life and Legend." *National Park Service*.
    August 2010. http://www.nps.gov/jame/learn/historyculture/pocahontas-
    her-life-and-legend.htm

Woolley, Benjamin. *Savage Kingdom: The True Story of Jamestown, 1607, and the
    Settlement of America*. New York: HarperCollins Publishers, 2007.

Further Information

Books

Carbone, Elisa. *Blood on the River: James Town, 1607*. New York: Puffin Books, 2007.
    Explore a fictional version of the early years of Jamestown through the eyes
    of a young boy.

Lange, Karen. *1607: A New Look at Jamestown*. Washington, DC: National
    Geographic Children's Books, 2007. Read about the 1994 archaeological
    excavations at Jamestown.

Walker, Sally M. *Written in Bone: Buried Lives of Jamestown and Colonial Maryland*.
    Minneapolis, MN: Carolrhoda Books, 2009. Learn how archaeologists have
    discovered more about Jamestown's history by excavating the graves of
    those who are buried there.

Websites

Historic Jamestowne
    http://historicjamestowne.org
    Explore the site of the original colony and see artifacts.

Jamestown Settlement & Yorktown Victory Center
    http://www.historyisfun.org/video/?cat=36
    Watch videos about recreating the time of Jamestown and nearby colonial
    settlements.

National Geographic Kids: On the Trail of Captain John Smith
    http://kids.nationalgeographic.com/kids/games/interactiveadventures/john-
    smith
    Play an interactive game that traces John Smith's journey to Jamestown.

Index

Photo Credits